T0162022

THE L NOTEBOOK

La Presse

PROVIDENCE & PARIS 2014

THE L NOTEBOOK
Sabine Macher

TRANSLATED BY ELENI SIKELIANOS

The L Notebook by Sabine Macher
Copyright © 1999 Théâtre Typographique/Sabine Macher
Translation copyright © 2014 Eleni Sikelianos

Published in the United States by La Presse
an imprint of Fence Books

La Presse/Fence Books are distributed by Consortium
www.cbsd.com
www.lapressepoetry.com
Library of Congress Cataloguing in Publication Data
Macher, Sabine, 1955
Translated from French by Eleni Sikelianos
The L Notebook/Sabine Macher
p.   cm.

ISBN 978-1-934200-80-3
1. French Poetry. 2. Poetry. 3. Contemporary translation.
Library of Congress Control Number: 2014932438

First Edition
10 9 8 7 6 5 4 3 2 1

We would like to give our warmest thanks to Benedicte Vilgrain and
Bernard Rival of Théâtre Typographique, who first published this work
in French, for generously allowing us to publish this translation.
Information on their press can be found at www.thty.fr

ACKNOLWEDGEMENTS

Grateful thanks to the Centre national du livre, which supported the translation of this book with a grant.

A section of this book was previously published in *Aufgabe*.

THE L NOTEBOOK

it's cold again

it's the day before easter

the computer lights up

the yellow rose is before me

everyone in the house is quiet

the hosts and the guests

i think of whom i thought of when i bought this notebook

yellow outside red within

of the shadow around his eyes

shadow in his mouth

i don't know his hands very well

i'm on the mezzanine with a daisy in an eggcup

i turn the first page of the *l* notebook

there are notebooks for everything

the left hand is poised fingers fanned out

a fingernail pins the page

the index curved like a claw to keep it company

i'll make no record of the hour or date

we'll bathe in the sea once

walk out into the foam

tonight the clock changes for summer and it's cold here in westphalia

notebook of *l* of lack

the carpet stretches out in front of me

my feet touch the ground without walking

my legs at right angles

i wait for the house to quiet down before calling

words of *l*

i think of him walking

i don't move

near the lamp

the second page is thicker than the first

the yellow rose seems to wilt before blooming

it's too hot for it on this side of the glass

the moth outside near it is cold

every evening i watch the tips of the dead leaves with their wrinkled

folds full of sparkling particles

i don't know what plant they fell from

we'd be sparkling and lovers

what can be done

i drink tea from a glass

the sun warms my chest and my eyelids

my arms rest in the length of their orange sleeves

the liquid's bubbles at the glass's edge gather when i tip it

to drink

love is love

the sun comes up behind the low wall

i write small

close to a blur

a bird sings

i can't see it

i don't know what color its feathers are

whether its eggs are speckled brown or golden bronze

the teapot i put into a niche has a shadow

i don't write to him

it's too early

first i must write to the paper

to the ink

birds with long beaks

judging by the depth of the holes in the butter

have eaten the paris butter and the bread from eurowings

the wings of europa in the beaks of villeneuve-lez-avignons

i'm in my socks at my new desk

i have folds in my face in the little mirror

around my chin and around the laugh lines that make an oval

from the wings

of my nose to the beginning of my chin

they recite too many lines here

it clogs the silence

dinner every night at a table of ten

then a walk through the dark to the pay phone

spring is veiled

my pants are too thin

the sun reaches into the alcove into my lashes

a rectangle of sun lies on the white of the bedspread

the orange is eaten

i cut it in quarters

a bit of flesh remains

flattened by my lips and teeth

attached to the skin

the bird came at dawn to eat the bread and butter i put out

for him at the spot where yesterday he stole it

the stone is hard against my back

the rectangle of sun falls across the notebook and the fingers of the

left hand holding it

the right hand holds the pen

the pen crosses the lozenge of the thumb and index diagonally

invisibly supported by the middle finger

placed on the ring finger

in the play of the sun i can see the entire ridge of my nose lit up

and even the arc of my eye

one foot is cold

one foot is almost warm

i'm folded into the alcove

at dusk the birds shout in the cypress in the little cloister

notebook *l* and notebook *o*

i am nun of the love of birds

the little finger

then the flank of the hand

rest on the sunday blue cloth of my summer wool pants

a man's garment woven of long-lasting thread

these trousers will be around long after me and whoever

they belonged to before is perhaps now beneath the ground

in another pair of pants

olivier toin was buried with his hat

the big hat that graced his head when the radiation made all its

blondness fall out

he told me: without love i live happily

the nearness of death had taken its place

he was full with it

i'm at the very little window in my niche

i fart out the strawberries more gorgeous than good

i slept in the single bed without leaving a dent

i look at the stones in the wall

a doorway through which one could have left has been bricked over

i've got a lot of keys to stay in the cell

my lover packs his love sack

we'll go over to the other side of the wall

i count the banknotes that my mother counted

before she gave them to me

as her mother had done before her

i put them away

my hair has a red tinge next to the carthusian rose

this is a place to flee from

i'll do it tomorrow

the sky is in the wind with asclepius's comet a croate

told me in german

i balance the white bowl on the right knee which touches the left

the lover arrives

will arrive tonight

my foot next to the board on which i sit profile to the little

window i open facing the alcove where i place the teapot

and the sheaf

of music paper with the song *i am a catastrophe* on it

the people on the teapot are there

the man and the woman

each exiting the entrance to their dome-shaped tent or house

behind them in a cup the fabric around the metal chain holds the tea

the sun's light on the paper in the *l* notebook dazzles me

i bend my knees and head to be in the wall's shadow

left eye weeping with bedazzlement

in the shower

a saltpeter grasshopper

a grey house cricket

leapt on my towel

maybe the white and adventure attracted it

the croate man told me about a nun near dubrovnik who was

walled into a tower after having lit the convent on fire

at high tide the sea came up to her stomach

for nine years

term of her death by this punishment

i wonder if low tide covered her feet

if limpets attached themselves along her legs

on the thin part of the shins just above the ankle

clarissa

l like the yellow and black leafhopper i brought

into my room with the rose

i write on the monks' toilet seat

how many monks sat here defecating thinking of heaven

i'm thinking of them

i'm sitting next to the hole

i looked in

it's right in the middle under the board

the board is new

the seat is of stone underneath

a circle carved out of the slab

it must have chilled the buttocks

the shit in the hole

i don't know how they cleared it out of there

outside the sun hits the top of the wall

it enters the room a little later each day

it seems like spring to me

a few hours before my escape

i know and my two accomplices know

the leafhopper must have fled into the wall

i have taken two photos

i say goodbye to the summer savory

i'll give my rose to the etruscan princess

i hear the clink of the stones on the path outside

i look out the paper-sized window

the pen i'm moving registers the temperature in letters

do nothing

the arms of love are ribbons

the legs of love are tubes

the trunk trembles

i write like the writer from here

i'd like to see v's lips move around the pearly teeth

they're not all pearly and one tooth is missing

it's that missing tooth that distinguishes him from his forebears

notebook of l and notebook of o

bed for the ink from my pen which so

dribbles on this page though it didn't the page before

maybe because i just gave it a bath

i washed my hair covered with cloister

tomorrow a train awaits and berries

is dingy and what you touch burrows

i position myself in the patches of sun under the windows

i follow them according to their illumina

in the end we won't be able to tell when what was written of l

if love can be written

under the feeble lamp

with the music from the refrigerator

an ambulance goes by

maybe it's the police

they guard us

machine guns of the very young conscripts of the capital

keep an eye on us

truce of love and of the journal

the child's slippers are under the couch

the glass fish are in the water

one can come and one can go

i contemplate the weave where the rug is worn

i think the word inkwell

i dive into the inkwell

i have none

such a small notebook at the end of my thigh

just before the knee

i'm sitting on a white bath towel so as not to sit on the

mottled beige and ochre carpet

there is no more tea in the tall cup

there's a bit of butter left on a small plate

i have taken two photos

one of my legs among the postcards

the other of the teapot and the stainless steel pitcher against the wall

after the photo i stay in the silvery light

the windows facing my window belong to the hotel

from the elevator i walk straight turning three times to the left to get to my room in the fourth corner

in baseball that's called a home run

i slept alone

the wind on the balconies as in the middle of winter

love stays and love goes

i'm hair-edged

v has lost his head

i give the big ficus a bath

vintscheggen is jealous

it makes him dumb

i am in kimono in silence

in the café molière

i'm in tours

at night i sleep in a canopy bed

i think of the love of others

how sometimes that too

keeps me far from them

some teenagers eat sandwiches and smoke cigarettes

a very pretty black girl with dreads braided around her head charms

a pimply white boy

two male teenagers have joined a third with long hair

who was alone at a table

he jiggles his leg moving his foot against one of the table's legs he quietly trembles

he alternates bringing a lollipop and a cigarette to his mouth

a man who looks turkish is speaking to a woman with disheveled

hair whose face i cannot see

the man's is deformed by obesity

the chin wide as the base of a pyramid has swallowed up the neck

his head sits directly on the torso's clothes

notebook of o and notebook of l

forget the l

it's raining through the frost saints' chill

the heart is in the heart

i am without knowledge in my belly's warmth

the red kimono with the white pattern lies in front of the open window

the neighbor bangs on the ceiling because there's a party

between her and me

on the fifth floor

a green gnat insect lands on the index holding the pen

v is in the city

i am in the house

i slip out to deliver cakes

on the way back a young man of mixed race african and the islands

says to me:

do you want to make love?

i say no right away but he was charming

i kiss v under the kid's bike

next to the strollers in the dark

plastic bags with groceries in hand

we must not go

i don't know where i am

i wait

i breathe

l unfolds in time

the windows have been shut again

we spend all day in bed

we sleep separately at night

most beautiful is hair

it's cold again

there is much to do

the mango is getting too ripe in the fruit bowl

i think of his hands and the toes on his feet which so often look like

fingers on a hand

we are together in the same city and separated by it

its south-west edge tucks him in

its north-east heart holds me back

the lure of *l*

young people pass in the street two by two

i wait in a café for the hour of our rendezvous

a svelte girl holds the hand of a man translucent from festive nights

a man with grey hair gets up

he was reading

i am waiting for the young v's asymmetric face

the barman splashes me with drops of hot water while

putting away the cups

the sun is next to my legs

i am elsewhere

the word douceur on the dishtowel from nantes that serves

as a napkin at breakfast

fell from an american poetry game on the fridge

i love everything suddenly

absolute *l*

the left big toe is wedged next to its counterpart on the right foot

the left pulls the right until i let go because i'm describing it

there is still a slight superimposition of the limbs

there is still a red strawberry in the indigo blue glass bowl

the teapot is empty

the dreams have been written

all sorts of wonders are in store this monday

with the rising moon and the young girl married through scheming

in ozu's movie

in the wedding photo you can see tradition doesn't allow anyone

to stand out

it devours the new beings in each generation

the mail scattered in the room awaits me

i get back to him

l l and so *l*

at night i feel it and the next day

it trails in the rain which stays in the clouds

i look into the courtyard through the slats in the blinds

i eat chinese sweets and i feel their transit through me

in the square a woman comes and sits next to me

she speaks to a young girl she doesn't know.

i left home without the keys

i have nothing to say

nothing to write

almost

the black mushrooms on the desk

delight me

on the desk's skin i write by daylight

the plants are soaked with water from yesterday's weather

i'm waiting to hear steps in the hall

then the voice and the head held upward

like a swimmer afraid of the water

v's life he's up to his neck in it

the peony has made some leaves to shade the whole balcony

the little elephant is standing up in front of my notebook

the washing machine faucet drips in the bathroom

i'm smoking under the clouds

the ink leaks from my pen

the pillow is rolled up in the bed i unroll

music and mexican shouting *arriyou* keep me up

eyes closed i call the police

that's the first time i've ever written i call the police

there is also a storm

gorgeous rumbling thunder and lightning

that's what woke me

i didn't call anyone

i got up to mop up the water

this morning i'm making movements while moving

the morning dance

i get the house ready for the day

outside the weather is a tepid soup

made for kissing

the peony keeps its leaves horizontal far from the stalk thanks to

its slender red stems

it doesn't suffer from rainfall

it goes so quickly

the water drips from my stockings and streams across the balcony

a taste of coffee comes with the heat

i hardly believe it

i step into the shade

the wilted chamomile rings a cosmos

my eyes are ringed with fatigue and red at their edges

the moon is already up in the sky that's still light

i'm thinking of you who is perhaps thinking of me

thinking is an ogre who never feels full

i lean on the book *to love to be loved* in order to write

a cloud comes and tucks in the full moon

i am in place on the couch

the room must smell of curry

i can't smell anything

the apricots in the fruit bowl are surrounded by strawberries

the grey hairs loop in with the brown

everything is intermittent and constant

the moon nude once again

i write at night

it's not here yet

i tasted the wine

it's too sharp from the air that was trapped in the bottle

v is at the louvre with his friends

we're keeping a distance

yet we're keeping on

dreams this morning

how the day took a bite of everything around

without answers without questions

i write to write

i dance on the carpet's beheaded fur

here we are

the wind blows

introspection

introspection

the cosmos grows

fatigue is behind the knees

i open the two notebooks

the white one and the nepalese

under the eyelids fatigue takes a rest

i forget *l* in the *l* notebook

in the morning

radio on in a life of love

i don't know if in this life i could (stand it)

dust all along each hair

and in the grooves in the wood of my table

a desk of *l* with two inkwells side by side

two computers

i'd like to invent a double desk

bear the movements of my lover writing

can we love that much

we roll by new houses

in the tgv bathrooms *l* is honored

everything is made for giving it and getting it

we exit together or one after the other

i can separate myself from him to write because he came inside me

in his way

with rings that leave his sex and travel in mine

i'm not sure he feels them

writing in the traveling window i see wheat coming up green

and maybe barley

high up a buzzard turns or another raptor

a horse eats whipping its tail

a bunch of cranes extract gravel from a clear hole

from a clear dusty hole

my hair is reflected in the glass and my eyes

grenoble's mountains get closer

a church clock remains in the village

i'm hungry

to eat grenoble or half

the pine trees of voiron

the yellow notebook on the blue of my dress

the sun is moving towards its set

i switch pens

v comes down the stone stairs and whistles in the house

i hold myself back i hold him back

parsimony and cruelty are in *l*

everything is still green late may

to not recognize you:

i'm on the spot with flat stones

it was made for me by someone after

after *l* after the acquisition of the house

i cut the plants that hold water at the roots of their leaves

i think they're thistles

little insects dance in the last light

i think of the fly that flew zigzag in the work room this afternoon

v has begun to chop vegetables for a ratatouille

the eye must come and the evening

i bought some honey

i held him close to me and far from me

the sexes stayed together in their savor and saliva as two

not a house

i'm here

he's there

we woke up together

i hear his voice better on the telephone than next to me

i have an image of the red couch melting

time melts images and your laugh at the end of the hall

when you walk away from my door

i'd eaten a clove of garlic to separate my mouth from his mouth

i asked for sleep

i closed my eyes on his eyes

one small

the other closer to the socket's threshold

he read me words written by a woman speaking for a man who's

looking at a woman at the counter

in a bar

they spend the night together

the woman hangs herself while the man telephones his wife or

mistress the next morning

that's just what one imagines

nobody slept together or phoned or hanged themselves

it's raining and i have to take care of the windows

the french windows

i eat everything sweet

even the easter lamb in marzipan

everything is common measure

the two lilies have opened their calyxes

i propped them against the window

during the heavy rain

there was thunder without lightning

i think of him who is elsewhere

inside the music as he says and inside small and serious things

i go but the metro stays

in the strasbourg-saint denis station

what's getting ready

a storm

the wind picks up

heat rises from the ground

how is that possible

the light

there are ants in the lilies

they march along the stamens' yellow-orange pollen

the aphids are still tiny and crowded on the buds

i'm here with my body gorged on fruits and cakes

correspondence is on hold and hand-written letters

come

a card from england today from the woman who said:

don't explain

i write her from the newsstand

he's nearby with his satchel and his face and his hands that exceed

his clothes

the body arrives throughout the encounter

he's the one who arrives coming toward me knocking on the imaginary door

he says:

i've come to get you for the big migration

but since you're happy here

i'll leave you

i follow but feel like leaving you

we talk talk talk

about the world

planes

insecticides

i look at the watch ticking in this abyss

i want him when he is gone

he makes love to me before disappearing

like the spider's husband

he does it with his mouth and his cock and his hands

i crush aphids between the sentences i'm writing

ants in the lily planter are sucking the cherry i planted there yesterday

i see its dark red flesh through the brown earth

while he talks i think i'll miss him later

he often says:

you'll get sick of me

i'm sick of what keeps me away from him

police sirens scream and voices from the demonstration surround them

it's so pleasantly warm in this street protest that we

hardly notice

as soon as we've each washed our crotches

we count the points of the wound again

of faith

the slate is bad

l sleeps when man is a dream

this one has a face that loses its axis when he lays it down

the mask no longer stretched over the ears

it gapes

it's been raining straight since early this morning

the roses fold under the raindrops' weight

i can't see what i write

an insect roasts in the halogen lamp i turn on in the hall

v sleeps in sleeping

sleep keeps us lost

or other

women speak of flowers and of love

i've seen it in performances

speak of something enormous

an enormous notebook of l

the smell of insecticide spread by the two pest control men is fading

we haven't made love in this room again impossible

we did it at his house on his yielding couch

there are fewer words love words

i don't miss them

we are in the sad pocket

a minute ago we laughed a little

i asked him: should we leave each other?

—do you want to?

—not now

almost all the black cherries have been eaten

the pits with the stems in the china blue saucer from brussels

i want him to leave

i'm going east

he's going to stretch out in the south

he has the keys to my house and his

you touch me

you turn me

you mount me at the hips

it's you who sees

my head is low

i close my eyes so close to the sheets

we play

the game shuts

miss me

you are my capsizer

i don't know when i love him

i know when i don't

before the end of the notebook

a little more than halfway

after châlons-sur-marne

abhorrent

the summer day is ravishing

trees with soft leaves close to the train

june leaves

i'll say the words

in july maybe

how many days for them to arrive in my mouth

the rims of my eyes hurt

it's the polluted room

here i am looking at the strasbourg station

lying in wait to photograph the ten to ten plane

clouds above the station

the loops in the rug around my feet

the plane goes by too fast

i rest in *l* laid to waste

in the café *the slaughterhouse*

a drunk man with a hideous face seeing me write asks if

i'm writing

always after love he tells me

after having made love you: he moves his hand right to left

fingers curved

quickly with eyes scrunched up

almost closed

he makes a gesture of writing

there should be a notebook of gestures too

i've heard his voice on answering machines

mine

his

it's here

l of all the notes in his voice

i don't have a lot to do here in front of the monumental station

i blow my nose

i don't know how i'm going to get up in the morning

in front of the window is a wall

i look at the white of the napkin i've hung on the chair

the blank hangs drowsy

i have nowhere to go wherever it may be

i drink a coffee at the italian café

where a young man tells outrageous fairground stories:

someone falls from the merry-go-round, the foot is twisted, the

slave-driver-boss with white gloves gives young girls 200 francs to

dance in their underwear next to the bumper cars

two girls facing him listen for a long time

now that they're talking i hear that they too have alsatian accents

i'm going i'm going to the tram the bakery the nearly empty theatre

one of the longest days is with me

v sleeps in my bed

i am delighted with him with his sleep

day

he opens the curtain

he walks in the hallway

he'll come here see me on the couch

he's the weasel of the bed

opening the door i smelled the garlic from yesterday's

tomatoes provençales which have

disappeared in our bodies

love is a day

i'm at its window

it rains more and more this summer solstice

i write on my thigh in orange pants

my foot in double wool socks pressed against the French window

i am the woman who is looking for work sitting at home

the indian cake sags in its plate

there is liquid that wasn't there yesterday

he is in his place without me

i am in my place with no trace of him

there are only his underwear which i move to the armoire

they're on the pile of pants

no one will go farther than home

the raindrops on the snapdragons don't dry

you sleep you sleep

a waterlily on the surface of the day

you are buoyed thanks to the yellow floats your sleep shows me

i make men sleep

it's my work

it's my delight to watch them from afar surrendering to my gaze like

kids

cats

dogs

bums

drunks

as a kid i watched over my mother's sleep

at nap time

the tiniest noise brought her from the room in a rage

i run for the metro and the door closes in my face

i wait on the platform

v also is waiting for me

what's in his fridge?

i'm bringing bread from my house to his

i'll probably spend the night

with him who says: i love you

yet i am against him

too when i get near

he showed me some photos

i saw that he looks like his grandfather

i saw his mother too

so despised

with the face of a daisy

and two grandmothers with pointy noses and tight mouths

and him with his arms in the air so fast you can't see them in the photo

standing up to step into the car i dropped my journal

a young man with long hair bends down to pick up the white notebook

from the ground

in the car he makes a ponytail while talking to his friends

he gets off at bonne nouvelle

a man sits next to me and moves nonstop

feet crossed

hands together

he moves his pelvis

his neck

his arms

his knees

at saint augustin

sunday night

the man says the weekend's going fast

that he's a gardener at the state home la dass

and if i lived in versailles

like him

he could help me

talking to him i noticed he's cross-eyed

i wonder what his help would be

i get off at franklin d roosevelt

all the trees of paris are here

i'm going to the theatre to meet v

a man invites me to his table where there is already a man

i sit down alone a few feet away from them

v arrives

he addresses me formally

it's ridiculous

he asks if i'm chilly

it's warm and muggy

it's summer

i take it too seriously

one should take everything but less seriously

i'll try to listen less and let him duke it out with wei yang cheng

the man at the other table says: you wouldn't be bored with us

i said i liked bored

without the d maybe

bore

there is some virginia creeper

night i kick you off my couch

after a tango class

i don't know how you got home

i wrote you so as not to call you, talk to you

to leave you thus

he disappears

i use the informal with him finally

he has to come get a few things

i've left nothing at his house

i think he wants to leave his underwear on my green pants

in the armoire

l in the armoire

l ends here?

it passes out

he leaves a few words on my machine

it withdraws

i haven't erased his old messages

it grows cold

nor the piano

i haven't washed his towel

i haven't put the box for the earplugs away

his toothbrush remains where he placed it

at the gare de l'est there was a rainbow

and here

in the courtyard of the building

or almost

at the horizon of the first chimney

the wind chills me

we are no longer who we were

we are elsewhere one from the other and i remember

so little of the whole

we used to make a date and stay together

now we make a date and split

i'm the one who's leaving

he's disagreeable

i toss him into the ditch

i give myself over to blows

to emptiness

to holidays on my balcony

he's in his cage in the fifteenth

we were on a bench

i spoke

he wanted to get close

make gestures

the head that nears the neck to kiss it

arm that goes around the shoulders and draws me close to the chest

close to your chest

i have a meeting tonight

he wants to know with whom

i don't tell him

it ruins ours

i leave and call him to say yes

as you wish

we'll see each other

then i get a pile of his stuff ready to go:

toothbrush

lip balm

earplugs

underwear

there are also two paper presents he never took

i don't open the cottage cheese in the refrigerator because maybe

once again

he'll come here

maybe not

that's what we'll see

we said it was as if

loose

love

and is no longer

he gets on his knees to kiss me

i put my hands in his hair

one pair of underwear is high and white

the other black stretched across thighs

i hold myself in the doorframe

he pushes toward me like the chinese explorer

i found a bedbug at the head of the bed and another at the foot

this morning

when love is said to be over it can begin again

i am where we were

in the house in the mountains

in the room with the low ceiling

in the dark bed

i am there with the tractor noise

in front of a peach and an apple that i brought from paris

by way of rungis

i called you but could hardly talk

in the morning a fly visits my face until sleep slips away

then the fly

gamebird to spiders

i vacummed up two

love is where?

in the pocket between your teeth

i am the edge of the world

lean in

his answering machine answers when i call

in this way i hear his voice

the moon in the sky and the july stars don't hear him

one day is another and it's night

i'm sitting on the floor

i hear the refrigerator's song

he may have heard other songs

that of the fly and bluebeard

his beard grows and rubs other cheeks

and his sheets

light makes my eyes tear

it's difficult to be self

gnats fly in small piles

air is in the air

he wakes up near the beltway

i've begun typing the beginning of this notebook although it's not

finished being written

the sky has clouded

i wait for rain

the flies prefer to land on my arms rather than on the flypaper i

put out for them

birds do the evening song with their little ones

we don't really get any ideas with these sounds

i have grapefruit in my belly

i feel its color

the neighbor comes back out with his tractor

i water with the wheelbarrow

oh we'll say

the wind goes in the trees

i smoke in the window

the sun is on the roof

i took the scorpion out to the stone blocks by the side of the road

a wasp comes and goes out the window

i think of writing you in chambon-sur-lignon

of writing this address on an envelope that you would unseal there

even though there is no longer a seal on envelopes

the lamp is blinding me

the ko bird says ko one last time for me

i'm leaving here and going where he can join me

summer is made for killing each other

the dead cicada is in the jar next to my table

a new leafhopper crawls up the window frame

i think of his chest and his skin of wax

i leave my place here to winged beasts without feathers

sleep comes over my belly and my hips

i write myself solo now in this notebook

i am in the other world

the world without *l*

with handkerchiefs

it makes me sneeze to be so far away

maybe i'll never come back

paris undoes its braids and lets its hair float in summer weather

clouds travel around the chimneys' round exits

there is blue between them

no one rings

we don't know who is who

which hand touches the other

which sex awakens from its millenary repose

it's not hot

it's flat and the bedbugs become flatter in their fast

my bedroom prepares to know no nuptials

a liquid will come to cover its underground world

with a chemical shroud called: SDK 3

i wait for him near where he told me the age difference makes no

difference

it's the softest of separations

the heat makes an oily bath of everything

everything you feared comes to pass without exception

Sabine Macher was born in West Germany in 1955, and has been living in France since 1976. Although she has a Master's in German literature, she has devoted much of her professional life to dance. She has danced with a number of choreographers and groups, most recently with Laurent Pichaud and Mickaël Phélippeau. Both these facts — a foreign tongue and a dancer's experience — can be felt in her poems, and have perhaps kept her from being trapped in a particular aesthetic or articulation.

She first fell in love with French as a written possibility when she read Marguerite Duras, whose ability to create depth through a seemingly simple, paratactic language she admired. Macher's own work at first glance reads as a notation of the quotidian in precise detail as the sensate body moves through space, but there is an accumulation of temporal complexity — simultaneity and rupture—that complicates the horizon as the mind responds to its surroundings. As in Duras, a rush of meaning unfolds from a seemingly flat ground.

Macher is also a photographer, and several of her books incorporate images. *Carnet d'a* was published by Théâtre Typographique in 1999. Macher's other books include *Le lit très bas* (Maeght, 1992), *Ne pas toucher ne pas fonder* (Maeght,1993), *Un temps à se jeter* (Maeght, 1995), *Une mouche gracieuse de profil* (Maeght, 1997), *Rien ne manque au manque* (Denoël, 1999), *Adieu les langues de chat* (Seghers, 2002), *Le poisson d'encre dans ma bouche n'est pas à sa place* (1 :1, 2003), *Portraits inconnus* (Melville, Leo Scheer, 2004), and, most recently, *Deux coussins pour Norbert* (Le bleu du ciel, 2009).

Eleni Sikelianos is the author of *The Loving Detail of the Living &
the Dead* (Coffee House Press, 2013), *Body Clock* (2008), *The Book of
Jon* (City Lights Publishers, 2004), *The California Poem* (Coffee House
Press, 2004), *The Monster Lives of Boys & Girls* (Green Integer, 2003),
Earliest Worlds (Coffee House Press, 2001), *The Book of Tendons* (Post-
Apollo Press, 1997), and *To Speak While Dreaming* (Selva Editions,
1993).

She is also a translator of contemporary French poetry; her
translation of Jacques Roubaud's *Exchanges on Light* was published by
La Presse in 2009.

She has received numerous honors and awards for her poetry,
nonfiction, and translations, including a National Endowment for
the Arts Fellowship, a Fulbright Fellowship, residencies at Princeton
University as a Seeger Fellow, at La Maison des écrivains étrangers in
Britanny, and at Yaddo, a New York Foundation for the Arts Award in
Nonfiction Literature, the James D. Phelan Award, two Gertrude Stein
Awards for Innovative American Writing, and the New York Council for
the Arts Translation Award.

Her work has been translated into a dozen languages, and she
has participated in a number of international poetry festivals, including
the Centre National du Livre's Belles Etrangères reading tour of France,
the Days of Poetry and Wine in Slovenia, the Barcelona Poetry Festival,
and Metropole Bleu in Montreal.

She has taught poetry for Teachers & Writers Collaborative in
New York and California Poets in the Schools, working in public schools
and with at-risk youth, as well as in homeless shelters and prisons. She
now teaches in the creative writing program at the University of Denver,
and is on guest faculty for the Naropa Summer Writing Program.

The L Notebook is the twelfth book in the La Presse series of contemporary French poetry in translation. The series is edited by Cole Swensen. The book was designed and typeset by Erica Mena, and the cover was designed by Shari DeGraw. The text is set in Verdana with titles in Trajan and Lucida Calligraphy.